Words from a Broken Girl

Lateesch Corner

Words From a Broken Girl Copyright © 2020 by Lateesch Corner

All rights reserved. This book or any portion thereof may not be reproduced or used in any manner whatsoever without the express written permission of the publisher except for the use of brief quotations in a book review.

Printed in the United States of America

First Printing

ISBN 978-1-943284-70-2 (pbk.)

ISBN 978-1-943284-71-9 (ebk)

A2Z Books Publishing Lithonia, GA 30058 www.A2ZBooksPublishing.net Manufactured in the United States of America A2Z Books Publishing has allowed this work to remain exactly as the author intended, verbatim.

978-1-943284-70-2

Dedication

I dedicated these words to the love of my life... she exposed me to her paradise..... the unconditional love, she was my inspirational leader for sure. You can Rest In Peace i got it from here.

Osrine Johnson my dear.....

Contents

Why Am I Terrified?	1
What's Crazy Is	2
I'm Grateful	3
Fruitful Forty	4
You Thought You Had Me Convinced	5
Black Boy	6
Love	7
Someone Better Than Yourself	8
It Almost Kill Me	9
Look at Her	10
What You Trying To Hide Behind That Smile	11
A Man So Fine	12
Polk	13
Run Away	14
Fat Bitch	15
Pull Your Panties Up	16
Stolen	17
Dark	18
Save Me	19
Daddy's Princess	20

You Don't Hate Me...	21
Who Is That	22
I Didn't Know	23
Sexy Vs Beautiful	24
I Was Dead	25
What I Miss	26
Black King	27
The Universe Got Me	28
Waiting On Him	29
Lonely	30
I Wanted	31
Waterfall	32
Light Skin	33
Bacteria Infection	34
Disdainful	35
They say	36
Well Damn	37
How to love my daughter	38
You Are Not Alone	39
Me	40
I See You	41
Trusting People	42
She Loves Me	43
Two weeks	44
He Touched Me	45
You Can Say No	46
What Am I Addicted To?	47
Who Knew?	48

Why Am I Terrified?

Why am I terrified of rejection?
The crazy thing is, you can't ever get what you want if you don't try .
But I'm terrified of rejection.
You never know, he might want you too.
You will never know because you are terrified of rejection.
You picture him in pictures with you,
but you will never know because you are terrified of rejection
They say, "shoot your shot", but what if he shoots me down?
You will never know because you are terrified of rejection.
I think he might be the sexiest man I have ever seen, but he will never know because you are terrified of rejection.
I absolutely can't breathe when he is around.
What does that mean ?
You will never know because you are terrified of rejection.
Just want to know how he taste with some ice cream.
You will never know because you are terrified of rejection…

What's Crazy Is

What's crazy is, I'm super special.
I'm special because I'm black.
I'm special because I can create life.
I'm special because I be knowing shit.
What's so crazy is, I just found this out.
What super special looked like.

I'm Grateful

When I think about how grateful I am, I get tearful.
I think about the people that come before me, that didn't make it this far.
Just to Name a few that I never knew, Robert Johnson, Tami Terrell, Otis Redding, Aaliyah……..
they say they were taking too soon, but were they?
Jimi Hendrix, Lisa Lopez, Bob Marley and Sam Cooke...
Maybe they graduated early.
Did you ever think of that?
Lyle corner Sr, Candice Nyan didn't get a chance to meet 40.
I'm blessed The Universe gave me this chance.

Fruitful Forty

As I sit here getting closer to the day I get promoted to fruitful forty.
I get more excited by the second, as to where this means I am going.
I am on my way to create a million things.
I have given life.
I have given happiness.
And joy.
Now it's time for me to create myself.
Fruitful forty,I am blessed and I am unconditional love.

You Thought You Had Me Convinced

You thought you had me convinced.
You thought you would abuse me with your words.
Now that don't make sense.
You almost had me convinced.
Hell, I thought you was all I could get.
A short stubby weed man.
Now that don't make no sense.
You thought you could convince me to play a part.
I am the lead in this life.
Nothing second.
You were mistaken.

Black Boy

I was blessed with that gift of raising a black boy......
Black boy, black boy
Do you know of your gifts?
Black boy, black boy
Do you know how blessed... you are?
They fear you because they can't understand how great you are.
What they don't understand, they try to destroy.
Black boy , black boy

Love

Learning what love means....
Loving unconditionally, is it possible?
Have I ever been loved without limits?
Is it possible.........?
I thought if you don't honor me, you can't possibly love me.
Is it possible that I don't know Love because I'm incapable of loving myself.
Hurting and breaking hearts of anyone who dares to cross my path.
You thought you were the one huh?
Couldn't be...
You can't possibly love me, until I learn to love myself...

Someone Better Than Yourself

You work all the time,
staying busy to hide the pain of your thoughts.
If you stay busy, client after client, the thoughts won't have time to creep in.
You are spineless, too scared to be alone.
What you are afraid of ???
Afraid to feel how you really feel about yourself.
What are you looking for?
Someone better than yourself...

It Almost Kill Me

It almost killed me not to be able to save you....
The biggest failure of my life.
I've gone decades with you by my side.
My Renberg lady didn't have to fall.
Now, I understand more than anything, the big heart break of my life has been the biggest lesson after all.
I will move forward doing everything in your honor.
My Renberg lady ain't gone, she just transferred somewhere higher.

Look at Her

As I look at her reflection in the mirror,
I'm concerned by her thoughts.
It seems as if she doesn't know her strength.
She feels as if she is missing something.
She is...
The love she is supposed to feel doesn't exist.
She keeps digging, begging looking for the self-worth in his eyes.
She can't seem to find it because she thinks It's buried too deep.
It's just not there...
It's not buried in him; it's buried in her...
How long will she dig, looking for what is already inside of her.
You will never understand yourself until,
you find what you are looking for inside of yourself.

What You Trying To Hide Behind That Smile

They tell me to smile more, but what you trying to hide behind that smile.
They tell me to smile more, but what's your plan?
They tell me to smile more, but I am.
I didn't smile for you because I can sense the bullshit you are hiding behind that smile.

A Man So Fine

Have you ever seen a Man so fine?
You couldn't touch him.
Yeah you fine, you caught my eye,
but you will never be mine.
you way too fine,
I can't even look you in the eyes.
I stay away from such creatures in order to keep my mind.

Polk

You ain't shit!
You just going to sit there on the porch.
With your dick in your hand.
Yellowish green oozing out the head.....
You say you want me to suck it like I do the candy in my hand....
4 years old don't really know if I understand.

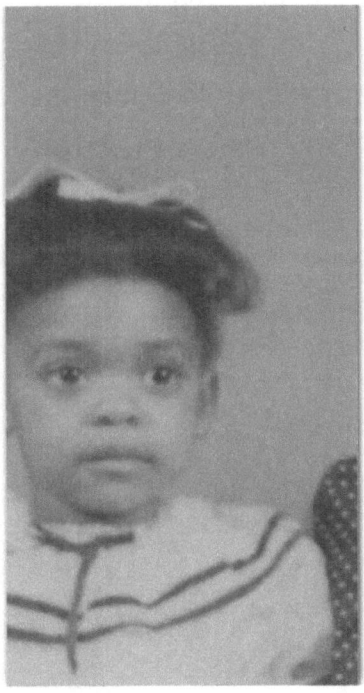

Run Away

I ran away thinking you would miss me.
I ran away thinking you would care.
I ran away thinking you would search for me.
I ran away thinking you would regret how you treated me.
I ran away because I knew that you would come.
You never came...
You never missed me...
You never cared...
You never looked for me...
You never regretted how you treated me...

You were relieved I was gone.

Fat Bitch

I been that.
Funky bitch.
I been that.
Stupid bitch.
I been that.
Nigger bitch.
I been that.
Black Monkey bitch.
I been that.
Tricky shape bitch.
I been that.
Lame bitch.
I been that.
Raggedy bitch.
I been that.
Rich bitch.
I be that!

Pull Your Panties Up

You are brilliant.
Pull your panties up.
You have a purpose.
Pull your panties up.
You deserve the best.
Pull your panties up.
You know this ain't right.
Pull your panties up.
You just wanted him to love you.
Pull your panties up.

Stolen

You stole my innocence.
You stole my purity.
You stole goodness.
You stole my righteousness.
You stole my honor.
You stole my honesty.
You stole my integrity.
You stole my worthiness.

You stole me.

Dark

Sitting in the dark,
I'm scared of what I might think.
Sitting in the dark,
I'm scared of what I might say.
Sitting in the dark,
I'm scared of what I might do.
It's scary being alone with your thoughts.
Never truly being free because your thoughts are making you a slave of what it fears you may become.
Sitting in your dark,
I'm scared of what I might think.
Sitting in the dark,
I'm scared of what I might say.
Sitting in the dark,
I'm scared of what I might do.
Sitting in the dark,
I will be safe if I just go to sleep.....

Save Me

You have spent your days waiting to be saved.
Since you were a little girl, you wanted to be saved.
But he never came.
You stand there in disbelief because you just want to be saved.
But he has yet to come.
So you continue fucking these nameless men, just waiting to be saved.
But he still has never came.
He ain't coming sis.
You have to save yourself.

Daddy's Princess

I can tell by the way he looks at me, that I'm daddy's princess.

I can tell by the way he tucks me in, that I'm daddy's princess.

I can tell by the way he brushes my hair , that I'm daddy's princess.

I can tell by the way he hugs me, that I'm daddy's princess.

I can tell by the way he is at home waiting for me , that I'm daddy's princess.

I can tell by the way he is always there for me , that I'm daddy's princess.

I can tell i ain't never been nobody's princess ....

You Don't Hate Me...

You don't hate me , you hate you...
You don't hate me, you idolize me.
You don't hate me , you crave me.
You don't hate me , you are afraid of me.
You don't hate me , you just don't understand me.

Who Is That

Who is that with those brown eyes?
Who is that with that soft brown skin?
Who is that with lips shape like a perfect flower?
Who is that with those elegant hands?
She moves like a love song.
As she walks by the glass she catches a glimpse of her sexiness ...
Who is that?
That's me.......

I Didn't Know

I didn't know I was priceless.
I didn't know I was valuable.
I didn't know I was supposed to put myself first.
I didn't know that I was supposed to love myself.
I didn't know I was important.
I didn't know I was royalty.
I didn't know that I was brighter than the entire sun.
I didn't know that I was perfect.

Sexy Vs Beautiful

Why do you say I'm sexy vs beautiful.
My lips are sexy.
My eyes are sexy.
My hips are sexy.
My breast are sexy.
My toes are sexy.

My love is beautiful.
My soul is beautiful.
My heart is beautiful.
My forgiveness is beautiful.
My being is beautiful.

I Was Dead

I was dead and you put the oxygen back into my corpse.
You gave me inspiration, something to hold on too.
How can you be a giver of oxygen and the giver of heart break?
You knew our history........
We trusted you.......
We believed in you.....
We wrapped you in love and you repaid us with theft of innocence .
You should really just end it......

What I Miss

What I miss most about you are our talks.
I would deliver the biggest problems of my life.
And you would solve it as if we were trying to figure out what was for lunch......
The strength and the security you always represented is priceless.
I know who I am,
because you allowed me to see myself through your eyes.
I know I am the gift.
What I miss most about you…. is you.
But you left me behind because I have so much to do.

Black King

They see how you hustle.
Black king.
That's the set up.
Black king.
They see how you hustle.
They didn't change the game
They change the rules.
Black king.
They see how you hustle.
Why you think they fronted us the cocaine?
Black king.
They see how you hustle.
They just made it legal to keep you a slave.

The Universe Got Me

Get your big ass on the floor!
You wanted me to drag your ass out the bed....
However, that's the problem you like being abused.
I won't help you beat yourself down....
I know when you let you tongue loose, you were speaking on yourself.
It's ok ......
you really hate yourself.
That's why you move the way you do.
Not respecting yourself or anyone.
You thought you would enter my world and change how I feel about me.
Nah
You see, I know what I am.
So that I'm clear,
She's someone you can't fuck with.
The Universe got me.

Waiting On Him

I've spent years looking for you in everyone I meet.
Missing everything about you, including your feet
No one knows how to take care of me,
like you did.
Why didn't you leave instructions?
No not none can manage to keep my attention for long.
Once I realize they're not you, I be gone.
I know you're here.
I can feel you.
Why do you insist on toying with my feelings?

Lonely

Why does it seem so lonely?
Wanting the touch of a man as I head home alone.
Wishing I was going home to a warm body in my bed,
but yet headed home alone.
No one to talk to,
No one to call.
I just want to fall, fall in love is all.
They say, "I'm not realistic at all' and that's ok.
I prefer the love affairs I have in my head any away.

I Wanted

I wanted to be a mother,
but I didn't sign up for this shit.
I have to buy them cloths and wipe they ass.
I wanted to be a mother, but I didn't sign up for this shit.
They ain't washing dishes or taking out the trash.
I wanted to be a mother, but I didn't sign up for this shit.
This is crazy, that no one ever tells you that one day you might not like your kids.
It's ok.
I'm telling you now.
I wanted to be a mothe,r but didn't sign up for this shit ...
go on a cruise instead ....

Waterfall

He says, "why you didn't tell me you had that waterfall?"
He says, "you trying to set me up with that water fall."
He says, "he never forgetting the waterfall."
He says, "I think I regret entering your waterfall."
He says, "I think it's a perfect fit , that waterfall."
He says, "it smells like fresh water, that waterfall."
He said, "you're quiet what you thinking .,,,,,"

That really wasn't shit

Light Skin

Ain't never been a fan of light skinned.
But it's something about that light skinned.
Ain't never been a fan of light skinned.
But it's something about how he stands.
Ain't never been a fan of light skinned.
But it's something about how he rocks a ponytail.
Ain't never been a fan of light skinned.
But it's something about how he says everything he needs say to say,
without saying one word at all.
Ain't never been a fan of light skinned.
but I think I'm going to give him a one way ticket in.

Bacteria Infection

What the fuck is that smell......
I smell like the juice at the bottom of the trash can.
I can't be well.
What does it mean?
Is it my body interrupting my days balance to ensure to me that something is very off....
Does it mean the person closest to me might be sharing themselves with someone else?
What the fuck is that smell, it just can't be right.......

Disdainful

Every time you come around, I want to frown,
but there is a smile behind my eyes.
You bring out a part of me that I never knew existed.
Making sure to protect myself from you.
I can sense that you want to take advantage.
Deep down I want to be your love slave.

However, I know eventually you won't mean anything to me.
I will capture you for a few months,
until I get what I need,
releasing you back to wild, he never knew It was me ....

They say

They say," why you mark up your body?"
I say
I covered my scars with artwork.
Disguise the pain that came from those scars,
those scars made no sense to me.
I was trying to have a conversation with someone I didn't recognize.
Trying to fix her just the way you wanted.
They said, "My nose was too big for a nose ring."
Now I have two, I showed you.
This is who I have always been.
Had to get over myself to become myself and I'm not even finished growing.

Well Damn

All this time I expected you to treat me how I treat you.
Well damn that was a disappointment.
All this time I expected you to miss me like I miss you
Well damn that was a disappointment
All this time I expected you to love me like I love you
Well damn that was a disappointment

When I started treating myself how I treated you
When I started missing my myself, like I missed you.
When I started loving myself, like I love you
Well damn.

How to love my daughter

How can I love my daughter?
When I've never felt love.
How am I supposed to know how to love her,
If I've never been shown
What to do......
I don't know what to do..,,
Unconditional love is the only love I want to pass down....
But I don't know where to find it......
Do I know that kind of love..?
Can you show me how to create it ......?

You Are Not Alone

You are not alone,
I want to be next to you,
I want to breathe the same air you breathe.
I want to relax you, like your favorite imported cigar does.
I want you to swallow me, like your favorite cognac.
I want you to hunt me, like you do money.

Me

I stand in the mirror respecting my blackness.
I stand in that mirror respecting this bone structure,
look how carefully I was crafted.
I find myself so alluring, it's hard to keep my hands off myself.
The more that I look,
The more I get turned on by the time that was put into creating and perfecting me.........

I See You

I see you watching me
Wising you were me.
Trying to figure out how I move,
Trying to figure out my beat.
Trying to figure out where my spirt was purchased.
I'm an original sweetie.
I can't be duplicated or recreated.
I move more because I can feel you watching me from the shadow.....
Wishing you were me.
Wishing I would let you in.
I feel you craving my spirit, craving my being.
I feel you watching me.........

Trusting People

Why do we blame ourselves for trusting people?
It wasn't your fault ....
You are supposed to love with a whole heart.
It wasn't your fault he couldn't be trusted........
it wasn't your fault he made you suck his penis at 5 years old.
It wasn't your fault they didn't believe you.
It wasn't your fault ....
Well, who's fault was it??????
They believed you,
but just didn't want to do anything to help you.

She Loves Me

She loves me with so much passion.
She took a piece of me that wasn't reachable by anyone else.
She loves me.
I can tell by the way she handles me.
She loves me.
I can tell by the way she caresses me.
She loves me.
I can tell by the way she sneaks to call me.
She loves me.
Well I fucked that up to say the least.

Two weeks......

Well I thought I would be down forever,
But it only took two weeks to forget we ever.
I thought the tears would never stop falling but all it took was a Pepsi and two weeks to forget your presence.
You thought you could cheat my heart with bullshit.
I've lost so much already that it only takes two weeks for me to forget your indiscretion.
Two weeks and I will have you replaced, please understand all it takes is two weeks and I'm brand new place ....

He Touched Me

I never thought it could exist.
He touched me.
Ooooh baby wasn't that the shit.
He touched me.
I love the way he sees through my bullshit.
He touched me.
I can't seem to catch my grip.
He touched me.
And gently penetrated my lips.
He touched me.
Ooooooh baby that was the shit.
He touched me.
Now I can't control the drip.

You Can Say No

They don't Teach us that we can say NO!
You didn't tell me that was an option.
They teach us to be lady like,......
They didn't teach us to say NO!
They teach us to eat everything on our plates.......
They didn't teach us to say No!
They teach us to do housework ....
They didn't teach us to say No!
You didn't tell me I had that option and now that I know , the answer is
HELL NO!

What Am I Addicted To?

Am I addicted to men, sex, or the idea of having someone love me.....
Screaming at the top of my lungs I want to be single but jumping from relationship to relationship with random hook ups in between.
What am I chasing?
What am I looking for??
Am I afraid to be alone???
Am I scared ????.........
Do I need someone to love me in order for me to love myself........
what am I trying to say?

Who Knew?

As I struggle to find my footing in this world......
Who knew?
Who knew the negative thoughts that would creep in my head?
Who knew??
Who knew that I would repeat history as I claimed I would never....?
Who knew???
Who knew losing my two biggest cheerleader would help me discover my spirit.......
who knew ????
Who knew that you have to love yourself more.....?
Who knew????

Interested in Writing and/or Publishing a Book?
Contact Dr. Synovia @A2ZBookspublishing.net

Contact information:

lateeschcorner@yahoo.com
Selfless_cuter (Instagram)
LaLAteesch Corner (Facebook)

Order online at barnesandnoble.com, amazon.com and other online retailers.